Reticulated Python as Pets

Reticulated Python Complete Owners Manual

Reticulated Python General Info, Purchasing, Care, Cost, Keeping, Health, Supplies, Food, Breeding and More Included!

By: Lolly Brown

Copyrights and Trademarks

All rights reserved. No part of this book may be reproduced or transformed in any form or by any means, graphic, electronic, or mechanical, including photocopying, recording, taping, or by any information storage retrieval system, without the written permission of the author.

This publication is Copyright ©2019 NRB Publishing, an imprint. Nevada. All products, graphics, publications, software and services mentioned and recommended in this publication are protected by trademarks. In such instance, all trademarks & copyright belong to the respective owners. For information consult www.NRBpublishing.com

Disclaimer and Legal Notice

This product is not legal, medical, or accounting advice and should not be interpreted in that manner. You need to do your own due-diligence to determine if the content of this product is right for you. While every attempt has been made to verify the information shared in this publication, neither the author, neither publisher, nor the affiliates assume any responsibility for errors, omissions or contrary interpretation of the subject matter herein. Any perceived slights to any specific person(s) or organization(s) are purely unintentional.

We have no control over the nature, content and availability of the web sites listed in this book. The inclusion of any web site links does not necessarily imply a recommendation or endorse the views expressed within them. We take no responsibility for, and will not be liable for, the websites being temporarily unavailable or being removed from the internet.

The accuracy and completeness of information provided herein and opinions stated herein are not guaranteed or warranted to produce any particular results, and the advice and strategies, contained herein may not be suitable for every individual. Neither the author nor the publisher shall be liable for any loss incurred as a consequence of the use and application, directly or indirectly, of any information presented in this work. This publication is designed to provide information in regard to the subject matter covered.

Neither the author nor the publisher assume any responsibility for any errors or omissions, nor do they represent or warrant that the ideas, information, actions, plans, suggestions contained in this book is in all cases accurate. It is the reader's responsibility to find advice before putting anything written in this book into practice. The information in this book is not intended to serve as legal, medical, or accounting advice.

Foreword

Owning a pet is a choice of many people. People like to have pets at their homes to have companions for them and their kids.

Sometimes, people want to own exotic pets. These people would want a sense of challenge in taking care of a pet. In this case, these people get the reticulated python.

This python, commonly known as the 'retic', has captivated a lot of hearts due to its muscular, large build, with amazing iridescence and beautiful patterns in its skin.

People have already retired the idea that this specie is aggressive and ill-tempered snake. They have regarded this snake now as a highly intelligent, easily cared for, and a very rewarding specie.

With any specie that you want to own as a pet, you will shoulder a big responsibility. You need to consider their needs before bringing them home. If you are not prepared with any responsibilities, you are better of without a pet in your life.

This book will guide you with the roller coaster of taking care of your chosen pet, Reticulated Python. Make sure you have thoroughly read the parts of this book before you go out and buy your pet. Let us start our wonderful journey!

Table of Contents

The "Regal" Reticulated Python 1

Chapter One: Reticulated Who? 5

    The Name Change and History 6

    Size, Life Span, and Physical Appearance 7

        Quick Facts 9

Chapter Two: Reticulated Python as a Family Member 13

    Why Own a Reticulated Python? 14

    Is A Reticulated Python A Good Choice of Pet? 16

    Money Matters! 17

    Budget Breakdown 18

    Housing Requirements 21

        Heat Sources 22

        Humidity 23

        Food Requirements 23

Chapter Three: Housing Requirements for Reticulated Pythons 25

    Housing Requirements 26

    Choosing the Correct Substrate 35

    How Often Do I Need To Clean My Reticulated Python's Cage? 40

        Cleaning Your Snake's Cage 41

What To Do When There Are Parasites? 42

Disinfecting the Cages 45

Where to Begin? Cleaning The Cage Accessories 46

What Do I Clean It With? 46

The Proper Disinfectant 48

Cleaning the Cage Quickly 50

Cleaning Tips 53

Chapter Four: Diet and Nutrition for Your Reticulated Python 57

Proper Eating Habits 58

A Separate Feeding Enclosure? 59

Feeding Amount and Frequency 60

The Correct Size of Food 61

What Should I Give To My Reticulated Python? 61

Pre - killed vs. Live Prey 61

How to Feed Pre - Killed Prey 64

General Feeding Guidelines: 68

Chapter Five: Starting a Family 71

The Basics of Breeding 72

Sexual Maturity 73

Mimicking the Environment 73

Male Interaction 75

    The Ovulation Process 77
Chapter Six: Health Care for Reticulated Pythons 85
    Common Health Conditions 86
    Stress for your Reticulated Python 100
Chapter Seven: Handling Your Reticulated Pythons (Optional) 103
    Can I Handle My Reticulated Python? 104
    Conclusion 106
    Glossary of Snake Terms 107
Photo Credits 115
References 116

The "Regal" Reticulated Python

The Reticulated Python, common called as the 'retic', is a popular pet snake species in the world. It is widely seen in Southern Asia, specifically the parts of Malaysia and Indonesia.

The Reticulated Python is a widely available species all year round. Imports of this species are pretty inexpensive but they might carry heavy parasite loads and they would have difficult time adjusting to the captive breed.

The Regal Reticulated Python

If you really prefer to have a Reticulated Python, it is best that you contact a captive breeder; they have healthy reticulated python hatchlings which would have better temperaments. Aside from that, they vary in colors and temperament.

A well - taken care of reticulated python lives from 12 to 20 years. Some snakes might even reach up to 30 years if you took care of it properly.

In taking care of the Reticulated Python, you need to provide the correct substrate, temperature, and lighting that would mimic its natural environment.

For the substrate, you can simply give a plain newspaper, some pythons adapt it easily. You could also give pre-cut corrugated cardboard, aspen, or even cypress mulch.

Aside from that, you should also give food to your Reticulated Python, because they are food loves. Most owners tend to give live food to this specie. But sometimes you can also give thawed or frozen prey items, or even freshly killed variants.

The Regal Reticulated Python

In the beginning, your Reticulated Python might not like to eat frozen or thawed food; you must inculcate this task into its diet slowly. Remember if you feed your Reticulated Python often, it would grow faster and reach greater length. Overfeeding could lead to health problems.

If you ever get a baby Reticulated Python, it would be very nervous and scared with giant predators such as humans all around them. They may even hiss or strike at any time. You should gently handle your snake so it can get accustomed to it. Before you even dream of touching your snake, make sure that the pet is not being fed so it will not be in shock when you touch it.

In this book, we will give you more details about these things in the upcoming chapters of this book.

Chapter One: Reticulated Who?

There are only a handful of animals that considers man as their food and the Reticulated Python is one of them. These snakes do not only exist to kill man, they are there to kill and feast on their remains. However, do not be afraid with what we have said because this python has greatly changed overtime.

These reticulated pythons have earned their man-eating logo due to their predatory traits in the wild; however, pet owners would argue that not all pythons have predatory tendencies.

Chapter One: Reticulated Who?

It is still up to your upbringing and history on how the pet would act. You should choose a python breeder that you know took great care of it to avoid unnecessary traits.

Pegged as one of the largest snakes in the world, this python could grow up to 20 feet in length and around 320 pounds! Imagine that! They do not really display aggression if you handle and train it properly.

You would be in awe due to its amazing patterns that 'reticulates' along their bodies. The beautiful patterns in their body are the main cause of the popular and commercial skin trade.

Do not be afraid, we will guide you in this journey if ever you want to own a reticulated python.

The Name Change and History

Today the common name for this specie is Reticulated Python, or shortened to "Tic" or "Retic", they are very prevalent but have changed names over time.

In the 19th century, the Reticulated Python was known as the "Ular Sowa". This name could be found in the British

Chapter One: Reticulated Who?

Natural History Museum especially its 19th century publications.

Nearing the 20th century, the python's name was changed to "Regal Python". People changed the name because it has 'king like' status in the snake hierarchy. The name fell by the end of the 20th century due to the increasing popularity of another snake, the "Royal Python". There was a big confusion between the species so the python changed its name to the "Reticulated Python".

The name was derived due to its patterns that looks like net that are found in animals, such as pythons. This specie varies greatly in intensity and color.

Size, Life Span, and Physical Appearance

The Reticulated Python boasts its massive 4.78 m and 170 kg average body mass! Some pythons could even reach up to 9 meters and would weigh around 270 kg! These pythons would have light yellowish to brown portions in their bodies that has black lines starting from its eyes and

Chapter One: Reticulated Who?

ends in their snout. There are also prominent black lines present in their head that extends up to their nape.

At the back of their head is a repetitive pattern of X that creates a wonderful diamond pattern. In younger species, they have latitudinal lines with black-edged spots on their bodies.

A great way to distinguish a Reticulated Python from its sibling species is by examining its upper jaw by the front part of the snout. For the Reticulated Python, they exhibit suborbital portion of the upper jaw, but it lacks a protruding or lateral figure.

For their species, females are much larger than males in terms of size and weight. A female reticulated python could grow up to 6.09 m and weigh as much as 90 kg! While the male grows up to 4.5 m long and up to 45 kg in weight.

In reality, this specie is rarely seen in captivity but more seen in the wild. The longest life span of this kind of python is up to 32 years. Reticulated Pythons who are in the wild have difficulty in finding food sources and environmental protection. A wild python could only live up to 23 years.

Chapter One: Reticulated Who?

Quick Facts

Scientific Classification: Kingdom Animalia, Subkingdom Bilateria, Infrakingdom Deuerostomia, Phylum Chordata, Subphylum Vertebrata, Infraphylum Gnathostomata, Superclass Tetrapoda, Class Reptilia, Squamata Order, Suborder Serpentes, Infraorder Alethinophidia, Family Pythonidae, Genus Python Daudin, Python Reticulatus Species

Distribution and Range: typically found in South Asia and Southeast Asia. Some can be seen in Indonesia. They can be seen in many islands where they can freely swim. Other than that, they typically live in woodlands and rain forest. They like to stay close to water sources such as lakes and streams.

Breed Size: large

Body Type and Appearance: The Reticulated Python ranges from 10 to 20 feet in length; some may even grow up to 30 feet. Their size still depends on the food and habitat that they are in. They have a very complex pattern of color that would enable them to fit in any surroundings undetected. Their colors could be black, olive green, white, and gold.

Chapter One: Reticulated Who?

Their body has a diamond-shaped geometric design that would attract any owners.

Length: they range around 10 to 20 feet, while some could even grow up to 32 feet long.

Weight: Males could weigh as much as 45 kg while females could be as high as 90 kg.

Skin Texture: slippery or slimy

Color: they have a complex color pattern. They contain saddle or diamond pattern with a black stripe that runs from their head up to their tails.

Temperament: The Reticulated Python are known for their strong personalities. Some might even brand them as "psycho", because they have not taken care of this species. In reality, there are many things that affect the temperament of the Reticulated Python, just like its history and its treatment. Its first nature is being a predator; some might even brand them as being the most intelligent snakes in the kingdom. However, these are smart creatures that, if properly taken care of will yield positive results.

Diet: They are constrictors, which mean they like to squeeze the bodies of their prey to inhibit their breathing patterns. They normally eat birds and mammals; some might even eat pigs and deer. If they have swallowed a whole and large meal, it may take your snake several months before it fully digests it.

Habitat: These Reticulated Pythons are typically found in places with nearby water such as the woodland or rain forests. Small snakes can be seen in tree grounds and shrubs, while some large adults are only seen at the ground.

Health Condition: The reticulated python is typically healthy but might experience common diseases such as anorexia, regurgitation, mouth rot, pneumonia, retained eye cap, and acariasis

Behavior: This specie tends to stay where there is a source of water. They use their body movements to defend their life.

Life Span: they live 32 years in captivity while 23 years in the wild.

These are just some of the basic things that you need to know about the Reticulated Python. You might still be hesitant to get this kind of python, but we get it, you might think they are still dangerous.

Chapter One: Reticulated Who?

Luckily, this book will help you in getting to know our lovely Reticulated Python. We will talk about things such as setting up its great habitat, substrate issues, food which you can give in its diet, proper handling and grooming, common health diseases, and some home remedies in case you got bitten by your Reticulated Python.

Do not worry; by the end of this book, you will know everything there is to know about the Reticulated Python. Let us begin our wild adventure!

Chapter Two: Reticulated Python as a Family Member

We have given you enough information about the rich history and quick facts of the Reticulated Python. The aforementioned facts are a handy guide about all essential things about our beloved python. We are just on the surface; we need to dive deeper into fully knowing our Reticulated Python. This chapter will deal with more information about the Reticulated Python: the budget that you need, traits, and necessary licenses and permits that you need to secure. You still need to know a lot of things before you go out and buy your Reticulated Python.

Chapter Two: Reticulated Python as a Family Member

You might think that taking care of a python is an easy task, but this is a holistic commitment that needs your full attention. This portion will deal with why you should own a reticulated python at this instant!

Why Own a Reticulated Python?

Having a pet in your life is an amazing idea, whether you want to add it as a family member or you will keep it as a companion. You need to know that purchasing your first pet will become a big and difficult decision for you and your household members.

When you have fully decided that you want to welcome a pet in your life, you need to determine what kind of pet you want in your house.

A Reticulated python is a good choice for novice snake owners. You might be scared at first, but you will just need to prepare some things and you are good to go!

Temperament and Behavioral Characteristics

The Reticulated Python is known to be an excellent

Chapter Two: Reticulated Python as a Family Member

swimmer and they could swim as far away from the shore at possible! They may be slow movers but they can cover big areas at any given day. These are nocturnal creatures, which mean that they like to move during night time.

They will coil up to you especially when they are in danger, because they are very aggressive creatures. And because they are heavy creatures, they can be easily found on land but some of them go into the trees. They also like bodies of water. If your snake is acting up, it is probably due to its stress and insecurity, so make sure that you deal with that! It could also potentially attack you if it feels threatened and unsafe in the environment.

If your Reticulated Python is born in captivity, it is less likely to be stressed from its new environment. They will know that the person who feeds them will never hurt them, and nothing bad will ever happen to them.

We have summed up all the behavioural characteristics of the Reticulated Python, there are so much more to learn! Let us head on the next sections to know more about our fierce but beloved Python.

Chapter Two: Reticulated Python as a Family Member

Is A Reticulated Python A Good Choice of Pet?

In this part, we will be giving more information on why or why not you should get a Reticulated Python as your pet. Make sure to reflect at each bullet because this will help you in your future endeavor.

Pros

- Reticulated Pythons are smarter than any other snake.
- They are more active than any other snakes.
- They are very easy to breed.
- This breed is easily available with many patterns and colors as their variations.
- They could live up to 25 to 30 years; you could spend a lot of time with your loving pet!

Cons

- Some reticulated pythons could be very aggressive.
- If you have a wild - caught reticulated python, it will have a very difficult time to adjust to their new

Chapter Two: Reticulated Python as a Family Member

environment. This might lead to accidental biting and misinterpretation.

- They live up to 30 years; you need to commit a whole life to take care of your pet.
- They are considered as Vulnerable, because many people are capturing this kind of python for their skin.

If you are now determined to get a Reticulated Python, make sure that you read on the remaining chapters to learn more about this beloved pet. However, if you are still hesitant, make sure that you still read through the book and see that it is just very easy to take care of a Reticulated Python.

Money Matters!

You have now made up your mind that you will purchase your Reticulated Python; however, there is still a list of things that you need to buy first before you even think of moving in your pet at home.

Chapter Two: Reticulated Python as a Family Member

A good Reticulated Python breeder would set-up a great place for the pet to stay, other than that, make sure to also have in hand food and some grooming tools that you need for your pet. Make sure to also have all the correct substrate supplies ready to mimic the environment that your pet will be staying in.

If you feel you can handle these tasks as well as spend much money on these things, let us move on!

Budget Breakdown

A new pet in your house would mean having a new companion in your life. You need to have everything ready at first before you even invite this new family member at home. You need to give the basic necessities such as shelter, food, water, and other stuff. For this task, you need to allot both your time and money for this.

You need to plan and track your budget for your Reticulated python, it will be very difficult at first, but you will soon learn the ropes.

The estimated spend for your Reticulated Python will rely on the things you buy, this includes the kind and types

Chapter Two: Reticulated Python as a Family Member

of resources that you plan to have.

Some things would be much pricier than other things because of its quality and number of stocks. Other than that, 'cheap' stocks are not really great for your pet because it might not have the same nutritional value for your Reticulated Python. Remember, cheap does not really mean that you save money from it.

At this part, we will give you a rundown of the things that you need to have to order to have a happy and healthy life for your Reticulated Python.

The Price of a Reticulated Python

There are many factors that affect the price of your Reticulated Python. Primarily, the factors are age and sex. However, the subtype of reticulated python also affects the price of what you want to buy.

Make sure that you will get your Reticulated Python from a trusted seller. In the next chapters, we will help you look for the best Reticulated Python breeder in the area.

Chapter Two: Reticulated Python as a Family Member

The subtypes of the Reticulated Pythons are as follows:

- ✓ Normal Reticulated Python
- ✓ Tiger Reticulated Python
- ✓ Albino Reticulated Python
- ✓ Motley Reticulated Python
- ✓ Pied Reticulated Python
- ✓ Super Dwarf Reticulated Python
- ✓ Ivory Reticulated Python
- ✓ Jaguar Reticulated Python
- ✓ Mochino Reticulated Python

Other Essentials

Aside from the Reticulated Python itself, you need to also purchase a lot of things as essential things your pythons would need in its life. These things are important because they will help your pet have a healthy and happy life. Remember, some of these things are just one time buy, while some things need to be purchase again and again because it will run out.

Chapter Two: Reticulated Python as a Family Member

You need to find the best option for your pet. This will not only help your pet live its life, but also for you because it will save up a lot of your money and time.

Housing Requirements

Captive bought snakes are better option that wild caught snakes. The former would adjust to the new environment easily while the latter would tend out to be more aggressive and defensive of its life towards other people, even the handler.

We think it is best that you only keep one Reticulated Python in one terrarium. We are not really sure how aggressive the python could be too aggressive in a different environment and with other pets around them.

The enclosure that you need to buy should be able to house giant snakes with great locking mechanism to prevent any escapes. Any small hatchling or baby reticulated python would do great in 10 or 20 gallon glass terrarium before you move it to a bigger and more permanent closure.

The suggested size of the terrarium for the adult reticulated python should be one and a half times the length

Chapter Two: Reticulated Python as a Family Member

of your pet. If your pet grows into the biggest variety of the snake, six to eight feet of terrarium would do.

Your reticulated python would grow fast during its infancy stage but the growth would slowly decline then stop all together. The price of a typical terrarium starts at $180.

Heat Sources

Your Reticulated Pythons are considered to be ectothermic species. They regulate their bodily temperature using the external sources of heat in their environment. You need to provide a gradient of heat in the chosen snake enclosure. This is done so your snake could choose what kind of temperature it wants.

The hot spot of the snake enclosure should be around 88 to 92 degrees Fahrenheit. The daytime air should be around 80 to 88 degrees Fahrenheit. Have a lot of thermometers ready with digital readout inside the enclosure. You should have one for the hot spot, one for the cooler section of the enclosure, and one for measuring the air. Have the thermometers with alarm that will go off if the temperature drops or changes this way you could be easily

Chapter Two: Reticulated Python as a Family Member

regulate and maintain the proper temperature.

During night time, you can allow the temperature to drop around 80 to 84 degrees Fahrenheit, just have a basking area readily available for your snake.

Humidity

Make sure that you have a ready water bowl for your pet Reticulated python. Aside from that, make sure that the humidity stay at 50% to 70%. If the percentage goes lower than that, it could potentially be harmful for your pet.

Food Requirements

Just like any other pet, you need to have a stable food source before you even think of bringing your pet home. You need to have a unique feeding regimen specifically for either raising your snake or breeding your snake.

The ideal food and feeding requirement for your reticulated python should just be the same with other python breeds.

Chapter Two: Reticulated Python as a Family Member

As a rule of thumb, Reticulated Python are voracious eaters and they like to eat live prey rather than eat prekilled, thawed, or frozen mice. You do not want your pet to have an injury due to a combative prey. Ensure that the prey is not moving too much before you give it to your pet.

Generally, pythons have heat-sensing organs which they call pits that can easily detect even the slightest change in temperature. You can soak your pet in warm water to slightly heat it up.

These are just some of the things you need to prepare before you have your Reticulated Python at home. These are necessary things because these will ensure that your pet will have a happy and healthy life.

We have just slowly introduced to you the things you need to have a happy lifestyle for your pet. Let us move on to know how to construct a proper habitat for your pet

Chapter Three: Housing Requirements for Reticulated Pythons

You have now fully decided that you want to own your first Reticulated Python. You also know its basic characteristics as well as its temperament. In the previous chapter; we have discuss the things that you need to purchase before you welcome your pet Reticulated Python at home. Before you purchase your pet, it is best that you have set up its housing need before you even bring your pet at home. Essentially, you will go through a series of terrariums as your pet grows up.

Chapter Three: Housing Requirements of Reticulated Python

Make sure that you have enough space where you can put the terrarium, as you will be changing it often. In this chapter, we will help you set-up and design your preferred terrarium.

Housing Requirements

Your Reticulated Python is exothermic specie, which means it will regulate its bodily heat through the heat it will get from its outside environment. Aside from this, they want a certain level of humidity to keep it hydrated so its skin will not flake out. Here are some things that you need to prepare for your pet's house:

- ✓ Cage
- ✓ Heat sources:
    - Incandescent light during the day
    - Nocturnal reptile incandescent light in the night
    - Tank heaters
- ✓ Light sources:
    - UVA light
    - UVB light

Chapter Three: Housing Requirements of Reticulated Python

- ✓ Hygrometer
- ✓ Foggers or misters
- ✓ Substrate of choice:
  - Cypress mulch
  - Paper towels
  - Indoor and outdoor carpet
  - Newspapers
  - Aspen shavings
  - Butcher paper
- ✓ Water bowl
- ✓ Plants
- ✓ Hiding spots
  - Branches
  - Shelves
  - Rocks
  - Vines

In the upcoming portion, we will help you set-up the correct housing of your Reticulated Python.

Chapter Three: Housing Requirements of Reticulated Python

<u>Cage</u>

If you plan to raise your own reticulated python, you need to start with the smallest size then slowly move up to the biggest size available:

- ✓ 10 to 20 gallon terrarium: best for hatchlings and baby pythons
- ✓ 30 to 55 gallon terrarium: best for slowly growing pets
- ✓ Custom built: this is best for reticulated pythons that are already adults

Reticulated python hatchlings grow very fast, so your initial cage might not be suited for it when it grows old. You can buy your own cage at a local pet store, just make sure that you choose an aquarium with a very secure lid to make sure that your pet will not escape, also see to it that it has proper air circulation and proper ventilation. If you are handy, you can also create an enclosure using melamine and plywood.

Chapter Three: Housing Requirements of Reticulated Python

Heating

Proper heating is required to maintain good overall health for your snake. All kinds of snakes require a temperature gradient that needs to vary throughout the cake.

Snakes need to regulate their own bodily temperature. They move to warmer spots to raise their body temperature, while they can also go to cooler areas when they need to lower it.

You need to include primary heat sources to have a maintained temperature throughout the habitat. Some primary heat sources include incandescent light during the day, nocturnal reptile incandescent light during the night, you can also put tank heaters and mat under the tank itself, and a great addition is the ceramic heat emitter.

If you already have a big enclosure, you need to use a space heater outside of the cage to maintain cage temperature.

In cooler weathers, you may add some secondary heat sources. These heat sources are used to create an even hotter temperature in a specific space of the habitat,

Chapter Three: Housing Requirements of Reticulated Python

especially the basking area. This area should be around 25% to 30% of the cage, other than that; it should be turned off during night time. Some secondary heat sources could be 50 to 75 watt of basking lights and incandescent bulbs. Other than that, you can create a specific hot spot using an under the tank heater on just a specific spot in the enclosure. Remember, you can't use hot rocks as the heat source, as this would burn your snake while using.

Lighting Equipment

Your reticulated python requires 12 hours of light as well as 12 hours of darkness within the 24 hour period.

For this task, you need to have two kinds of lighting in the cage, a specific light to provide heat, such as full spectrum fluorescent light that will supply UVA and UVB light and incandescent bulbs.

UVB lights are used to promote the proper synthesize of Vitamin D3, as a result, this vitamin will allow their bodies to have a proper metabolism of minerals and vitamins. Remember to turn off these lights unless you will

Chapter Three: Housing Requirements of Reticulated Python

buy special nocturnal lights that would not really emit any visible light.

When you purchase your incandescent light, make sure to consider the bulb's wattage. If you buy a bulb with high wattage, this will raise the temperature as well as produce more heat.

There are many heat sources that you can use; here are some things that you can use as heating device for your Reticulated Python:

- ✓ **Pig Blankets.** These are big heating pads that are enveloped with rigid plastics. These things emit high surface heat over a big area, and can be easily controlled by thermostats. A down side for this choice is this can be also bought at feed stores or reptile specialty places. In reality, these are the best commercially produced heating things for big reptiles.

- ✓ **Space heaters and room heaters.** If you plan to have a big snake collection or a room dedicated especially to your Reticulated python, you can do this task.

Chapter Three: Housing Requirements of Reticulated Python

Remember, do not place the heater too close to the cages, and do not let these things overheat.

- ✓ **Tapes and heat pads.** This is thought to be the easiest way to heat the snake cages. Just remember to connect it to temperature probes and thermostats.

- ✓ **Ceramic Heaters.** These are used as overhead heat sources but needs to have correct wattage bulbs and strong ceramic bases that are able to handle the wattage. If you choose plastic sockets with cardboard liners, it would burn just after a few hours. Just like any other choice, you need to use rheostats or thermostats for regulation. Make sure to cover the bulb with cage guard to prevent your snake from being too close to the heat.

Humidity

To maintain the correct level of humidity, make sure that you have available fogger or misters to keep the habitat moist. Other than that, a hygrometer would make sure that the heat level is not too low or too high.

Chapter Three: Housing Requirements of Reticulated Python

Make sure that you research thoroughly on the correct humidity level of your pet before you decide set up your misters.

Substrate

Each substrate will vary greatly on the specific specie, there are a lot of things that you need to consider before you even purchase on.

First, you need to make sure that the pet will not ingest the substrate of your choosing, aside from that, make sure that you know the humidity requirements of your pet.

Common substrates include paper towels, cypress mulch, newspaper, indoor/outdoor carpet, butcher paper, and aspen shavings.

Accessories, Plants, and Other Decorations

Some common items that you can put inside the cage are hiding spot or shelter, water bowl, rocks, branches, and shelves. These will mimic the natural environment of your pet.

Chapter Three: Housing Requirements of Reticulated Python

The water bowl is essential for your pet because the reticulated python needs to drink and soak. Aside from this, the water would aid to maintain the humidity level in the habitat.

A hiding spot would be used by your pet snake as a place to rest as well as a place for it to have a sense of security. You can use a flower pot, a large box, or any other item that would create a blackout environment. The hiding spot should be big enough so your pet Reticulated Python could fit itself. If you are unable to do this, your pet would feel vulnerable and exposed and soon become stressed. A stressed out python could easily contract disease because of a stressed immune system or even self-injury.

Places to climb and rest could be branches, vines, shelves, and other similar items. You can also use rocks or branches as scratching spots for your pet. These will be used by your skin when it is shedding its skin. These should be rough, but not too abrasive.

Your chosen pet, the Reticulated Python, is a big snake. It can easily destroy and fragile decorations or any small living plants that you will put inside the enclosures.

Chapter Three: Housing Requirements of Reticulated Python

Choosing the Correct Substrate

Snakes are a great choice as your pet; you just need to choose the correct type and a healthy reptile breed. You need to put your snake in a properly sized and secure cage that is made from strong material, and it must be secured with a lid.

We will provide you with several kinds of substrate that you can use for your Reticulated Python. We will also give you the pros and cons and then choose the best type to use for the Reticulated Python.

- ✓ Newspaper

This is a popular choice to be the snake bedding because it is easily available around the area. Usually, you can get these things for free and can easily be changed if your pet wets it. Remember, your snake could not burrow or hide in these things. Aside from this, this is not really pleasant to look at, but this is a great choice if you have a tight budget.

Chapter Three: Housing Requirements of Reticulated Python

✓ Paper Towels

These make good Reticulated Python bedding because they can easily absorb moist and can be easily replaced when soiled, just like the newspaper option.

You just need to remove the towels and replace with new towels when you are cleaning the cage of your snake. However, this option is only viable if your snake does not burrow or hide too much.

✓ Sand

Among all the choices, the sand is the most aesthetically pleasing option for the substrate for your snake, comparing to paper towels or newspaper. You can easily purchase this in pet shops in varied colors that could fit any design of your home.

Your Reticulated Python could easily burrow in this kind of substrate but your snake could possibly swallow the sand. If ingested, this would cause impaction and the grains of the sand could possibly get under the scales of your Reticulated Python. Other than that, this kind of substrate will get soiled easily and needs to be replaced immediately.

Chapter Three: Housing Requirements of Reticulated Python

You need to determine if the visual appeals weighs more than the initial problem.

✓ Carpeting

This kind of substrate is one of the best choices for non-burrowing snakes. It may be cheaper if you only use remnants, but you need to provide at least two pieces of big sizes that would fit in the cage.

You can alternate the two carpets while you wash the other carpet. This kind of substrate gets soiled easily, so this you need to frequently wash your carpets.

✓ Artificial Turf

This kind of substrate is the same as carpets. You can own multiple pieces so you can constantly swap pieces while you are cleaning the dirty one. Unlike the carpet, this turf is very easy to clean. Aside from that, this will last a long time and also durable, however, the appearance will surely deteriorate due to wear and repeated washing.

This mimics real grass so your snake could have a good time in this kind of substrate, but they could not really

Chapter Three: Housing Requirements of Reticulated Python

burrow in this kind. You can easily buy this in a home improvement store and cut it in small pieces that would easily fit your pet's cage.

✓ Cypress Mulch

The Cypress Mulch is considered to be the most comfortable substrate for your pet Reticulated Python. Your pet could easily dig inside the much while still retaining humidity. It is very beautiful and has a pleasant but not a very powerful smell. This kind of mulch is relatively cheap and easily available at garden shops. You just need remove the mulch in order to clean the cage of your Reticulated Python.

You need to bake your cypress mulch in the over for around 30 minutes before you use it as your snake bedding. This task would kill mites and any other insect that might live among the mulch.

✓ Aspen Shavings

Aspen shavings make great substrate for your Reticulated Python unlike pine shavings and cedar. You can

Chapter Three: Housing Requirements of Reticulated Python

use this kind of shaving even for small snakes and those that would not need high humidity. A word of caution, this kind of shaving would get moldy if it has too much moisture, aside from that, particles could go under the scales of your snake, especially on its belly - which might cause irritation.

This is easily available at your local pet stores because this is one of the popular substrate type for different kinds of pets, which would include rats, rabbits, mice, and guinea pigs.

✓ Coconut Fiber Bedding

The coconut fiber bedding is a soft fiber and comfortable bedding choice for your snake and any other reptiles. This substrate contains natural odor fighting properties and your snakes could easily burrow in this kind of bedding. You can easily find this in any pet stores near you. These are just some of the substrate types that you can choose from for your Reticulated Python's bedding. There are a lot of other choices out there, but we believe this is the best among the rest. We hope we have helped you make the decision on the type of substrate that you can use.

Chapter Three: Housing Requirements of Reticulated Python

How Often Do I Need To Clean My Reticulated Python's Cage?

Your Reticulated Python needs to have a clean place to live, with no rotten food, no feces lying around, and no dangerous bacteria lurking around. However, frequent cleaning of the cage could be unnerving and stressful for your python. You need to set your cleaning time to minimize your Reticulated Python's stress.

Good Cleanliness

While in the wild, your pet Reticulated Python's habitat is easily cleaned with rain showers, air circulation, change of season, and life cycle of both animals and plants. However, when in captivity, your pet could not really rinse itself by diving in stream, go to a clean region while the nature is cleaning its dead skin.

You need to be the one to clean after your pet or else there will be unpleasant consequences, just like:

- ✓ Any unpleasant and strong smell from the dirty cage or tank
- ✓ Less fun and enjoyment in the closure

Chapter Three: Housing Requirements of Reticulated Python

- ✓ You can't see where your pet due to poor visibility is.
- ✓ Quick spread of harmful bacteria that might be easily transmitted to humans
- ✓ Sudden change in your Reticulated Python's behaviour such as lethargy and aggression.
- ✓ Illness, signs of discomfort, and even death.

Do not fret; cleaning your Reticulated Python's cage is just an easy task, especially if you have correct timing.

Cleaning Your Snake's Cage

There are many factors that would affect how much or how often you need to clean your Reticulated Python's cage or tank. A Reticulated Python is big specie yet it is not that active.

When you clean, make sure that you look for specific signs that your Reticulated Python may be ill. Also, watch out for these things from the cage and correct or remove them.

Chapter Three: Housing Requirements of Reticulated Python

Ask yourself:

- ✓ Was the correct amount of food eaten by my Reticulated Python?
- ✓ Is the temperature bearable for my Reticulated Python?
- ✓ Are then urates and feces inside the cage? Are they within normal appearance and quantity?
- ✓ Is there any skin shedding? Do they appear normal?
- ✓ Are there parasites presents?

What To Do When There Are Parasites?

Mites often appear as small brown, black, or red spots around your pet's scales, eyes, or even moving over the skin.

Ticks, on the other hand, are larger, appears to be black, brown, or gray in color. Internal parasites can be seen through grave changes in feces or emaciation.

Here are the tasks that you need to do whenever you are cleaning your reptile's cage:

- ✓ **Daily Clean-up.** There are certain things you need to clean but make sure to not stress your pet whenever you are cleaning. Any food and water dishes left for the day

Chapter Three: Housing Requirements of Reticulated Python

should be cleaned and replenished daily. Aside from that, any uneaten food should be removed by the end of the day. Shed skin should be removed before it creates an even dirtier environment. Make sure you do this carefully yet quick as not to disturb your pet easily, this would keep a nice and healthy environment for your pet.

- ✓ **Weekly Clean-up.** A thorough clean up once a week is enough for most habitats. For this time, almost all surface area should be wiped carefully with the chosen disinfectant; rocks and woods should also be removed and wiped down. Decaying and dead plants should be removed as well as other fixtures and toys. A dirty substrate should be either removed or cleaned. To finish this task, you need to temporarily remove the Reticulated Python in the cage so it would not be disturbed by your activities.

Chapter Three: Housing Requirements of Reticulated Python

- ✓ **Monthly Clean - up.** The monthly clean-up is considered to be a deep cleaning. However, you should not do this frequently for some specie. In this type of cleaning, remove everything from the habitat and make sure that all surface area should be scrubbed; you need to also scrub the corners of the cage with a toothbrush. You should also change all the substrate. Dishes, woods, and rocks should be thoroughly soaked with disinfectant or replaced. Air dry the enclosure until there is no cleaning fumes seen from the cage, this task should take you about a couple of hours. You could add new toys or even rearrange the habitat that would provide a better mental challenge to your Reticulated Python. While you are doing this, make sure that your pet is in a safe, temporary home until you have finished the deep cleaning and came out with a refreshed habitat.

After these tasks, do not forget to clean your hands with hot, soapy water. You do not want to be infected with whatever affects your pet.

Chapter Three: Housing Requirements of Reticulated Python

Cleaning your pet's cage is an essential task owning and caring for your pet. Realize that proper timing is a vital thing for your cleaning task.

Disinfecting the Cages

The cage of the Reticulated Python needs special care in order to be always clean. You need to routinely maintain the cage is needed to have a healthy and safe home for your retic. The enjoyable, odor - free, attractive cage is also for your enjoyment.

Your pet is very susceptible to bacterial and skin infection. The housing and cage should be neatly and squeaky clean. Their fecal matter carries tons of bacteria, such as Salmonella, this may be easily transmitted to you, through the cage, furnishing, and even the cleaning equipment. In order to prevent this, you need to regularly clean the cage and periodically disinfect the materials that you are using.

Chapter Three: Housing Requirements of Reticulated Python

Where to Begin? Cleaning The Cage Accessories

Make sure that all living things, such as branches and rocks that you will put into the habitat are sterile.

The rocks that you will put in the cage should be cleaned; you can boil this in water for 30 minutes. The sand could be rinsed with large amounts of water in order to remove the debris, and then heated in the oven for 30 minutes. This task is also applicable to branches, and you also need to heat this in your oven.

What Do I Clean It With?

You need to put together a cleaning kit when you clean the cage of your Reticulated Python. Put these items separately from your other household items. This task is to prevent cross-contamination, do not use tubs or sinks that you also use for human bathing or even food preparation. Here are some useful things that you can purchase:

- ✓ Back-up terrarium - this is a sterile environment for the amount of time that you will put your snake whenever you are cleaning its official cage.

Chapter Three: Housing Requirements of Reticulated Python

- ✓ Brushes - you may purchase small and medium size, this well depends on your cage. You also need to have a toothbrush to clean the crevices of the decoration and the corners.

- ✓ Buckets

- ✓ Terrarium cleaner - this is used to dissolved hardened matter

- ✓ Paper towels

- ✓ Toothpicks, razor blades, Q-tips, and putty knives - these are purchased to reach the smallest of place and even to remove any small hardened material.

- ✓ Rubber gloves and goggles

- ✓ Sand-sifter - this is used to remove debris and feces from sand or other sand-like substrate

Chapter Three: Housing Requirements of Reticulated Python

- ✓ Commercially available soap or dish washing detergent - This is great for cleaning surfaces but you should not use any products that contain pine scent or phenol.

- ✓ Sponges - Use a specific sponge for rinsing and disinfecting. Make sure that you do not cross contaminate the products.

When you are cleaning, make sure that you are using latex or rubber gloves as well as protective goggles. Even every time you are holding your python, or even a tiny cleaning procedure, you should wash your hands thoroughly. You could also use a hand sanitizer.

The Proper Disinfectant

You need to choose the proper disinfectant for cages. This task should be done very carefully. The disinfectant of your choosing should be strong enough to kill any disease-causing bacteria, fungi, and even viruses. However, these things should not harm your Reticulated Python. Remember, your retic is very sensitive to toxic fumes so you

Chapter Three: Housing Requirements of Reticulated Python

need to take care and move them to a different room while you are using the disinfectant.

There are many commercially available disinfectants in the market. One of the most readily available disinfectants for cleaning your reptile's enclosure is a household bleach. Make use of a bleach in a diluted form. The parts should be 1 part bleach and 32 part water. Some disinfectants might be available at your vet's office.

Remove feces, soaps, food, and any other material before you disinfect. Any presence of organic material would prevent it to work. Clean all he soiled areas of the cages, its accompanying accessories. You can use a solution of hot water and dish washing liquid. Make sure to disinfect and rinse well.

Apply your disinfectant liberally to the accessories and the cage. Let the disinfectant sit for around 10 minutes. If the material is very porous, you may need to allot longer time.

After this, rinse well, especially the wooden items, make sure you thoroughly clean it with water to remove all traces of disinfectant.

Chapter Three: Housing Requirements of Reticulated Python

For your own comfort and safety, use the bleach in a well-ventilated safe area. Use goggles and rubber gloves when you are doing this.

Allow your cage and all the items to be dried thoroughly before you assemble all the pieces and placing back your Reticulated python, assembling and placing the herp back into the cage.

Cleaning the Cage Quickly

Here are the recommended steps when you are cleaning your cage:

1. Put all your paper towels, water bottle / sprayer, disinfectant, trash bag, and other materials ready for use.

2. Place your pet in a temporary holding area. You can use a medium-sized sterile box with a lockable lid and air holes.

3. Remove all the pieces of furniture, such as hiding spots, bowls, and etc. Place them in a utility sink or in bathtub.

Chapter Three: Housing Requirements of Reticulated Python

4. Unplug all the electrical devices on the cage, such as the lighting and heating lamps.

5. Remove the substrate from the cage.

6. Empty the cage thoroughly. Spray the cage with water and wipe with paper towels, get all the dust, visible matters, and all the dust. Go over it a couple of times with an antibacterial disinfectant product.

7. Do not spray cold water on a hot glass. For example, you are spraying the bottom of the terrarium with heat pads. This task would lead to a cracked glass. Cool the glass a bit before cleaning it.

8. Leave the cage open so all the air can go out and dry completely, do this while you are cleaning the furniture.

9. When cleaning the cage item, you can use any antibacterial soap and a dose of hot water. If you see that the furniture is very dirty, you may need to soak it

Chapter Three: Housing Requirements of Reticulated Python

overnight in a diluted bleach solution. However, if you clean the cage on a daily basis, using bleach is not that necessary.

10. Pay special attention to the water bowl. Clean it with hot water and antibacterial soap. Repeat this process twice, then rinse it with hot water.

11. Do not scrub plastic bowls with scouring pads or fingernails. This action will leave scratches and abrasions; this would then lead to more difficulty in cleaning the items. Bacteria would more likely breed from pitted or scratched surfaces, because they are more difficult to clean. Use the smooth part of your finger to thoroughly clean the bowl or even soak it overnight.

12. Place back new substrate, furniture, and replenish the bowl with fresh water, then place back your pet.

13. When everything is back in place, plug in the electrical devices. Check all the locks and latches.

Chapter Three: Housing Requirements of Reticulated Python

Cleaning Tips

Here are some cleaning tips that will help you save time and energy and might even help to lengthen your cage's life.

- ✓ Blue, thick paper towels are great for cage cleaning as well as snake maintenance.

- ✓ Have an extra set of cleaning supplies read to be used during emergencies or even when you run out of it. You need to have extra cleaning spray, substrate components, paper towels, and etc.

- ✓ Have a pump dispenser of sanitizer ready near the cage of your Reticulated Python. Use it before and after you handle the snake, and frequently while you are cleaning the cage. The sanitizer will protect both you and your pet for possible cross contamination.

Chapter Three: Housing Requirements of Reticulated Python

- ✓ A simple set-up is easy to clean. Have a balance of simplicity and visual appeal that works best for you. A naturalistic cage may be visually appealing, but more difficult to clean.

- ✓ Your cages have edges that are very difficult to clean. Possibly, you need to buy an enclosure that has rounded edges. These are easier to wipe and clean.

- ✓ When water from your water bowl evaporates, there are mineral deposits left on the bowl itself - this will be very difficult to remove. You need to constantly clean and refill the bowls so you will not have deposits stuck on the bowl.

- ✓ After cleaning the cage, you can put a tasty snack on the cage for your pet! Clean habitat plus a nice treat makes a happy and healthy snake.

Chapter Three: Housing Requirements of Reticulated Python

These are just some things that you need to remember when setting up a habitat for your Reticulated Python. These are basic reminders that you need to follow so you and your pet will not contract any harmful diseases.

Chapter Three: Housing Requirements of Reticulated Python

Chapter Four: Diet and Nutrition for Your Reticulated Python

Food is an important part of any living being. Food will help your pet have a happy and healthy life. Your Reticulated Python is just like other animals, they need food to have nutrients in their body and have a long life.

Feeding your Reticulated Python is not an easy task; it is not that easy unlike dog or a cat. This will involve more than just placing a bowl of food to your Reticulated Python.

In this chapter, we will help you determine the proper diet for your Reticulated Python.

Chapter Four: Diet and Nutrition for Reticulated Pythons

We will also deal with how to feed pre-killed, thawed, or even fresh prey to your Reticulated Python. Do not be afraid because we will help you in this task.

Feeding your Reticulated Python is not an easy task. You need to put time and effort as well as the correct methods. This would make a happy and well-nourished life.

In their natural habitat, the Reticulated Python almost always eat warm-blooded preys such as waterfowl, nesting birds, pigs, deer, rodents, and other same mammals. Retics are known to be opportunistic feeder, which means they likely eat animals that have died recently.

Proper Eating Habits

You first need to make sure that your snake eats properly through setting up and maintaining the correct habitat. Every species has its own unique requirements that concern lighting, temperature, humidity, accessories, layout, size of habitat, and others.

Chapter Four: Diet and Nutrition for Reticulated Pythons

If your snake lives in an environment that is too dark, too cold, too small, or improperly maintained will have a decrease of appetite while some might not really eat.

Have your habitat ready before you bring your snake home and monitor with hygrometers, thermometers, timers, and other helpful equipment.

A Separate Feeding Enclosure?

You may want to have a separate enclosure that is only for feeding, it is not that necessary, but will be somehow helpful. If you will use a different enclosure for feeding, it will keep your main cage more sanitary and so much cleaner.

A separate feeding habitat will only be necessary if you have more than one snake; this would lessen the chances of being the other snakes as prey as well as keeping the substrate from being ingested.

Chapter Four: Diet and Nutrition for Reticulated Pythons

Feeding Amount and Frequency

You only need to feed your Reticulated Python during its active times. Research your Retic's behavior or you can ask your vet to determine when is the best time to feed your snake.

The amount of food that you feed your Reticulated Python well depends on the specie and the age. Baby snake will not really look for food unless it is only two to four weeks of age.

Young snakes need to eat around twice a week, or every 2 to 7 days. The frequency will depend on how quickly you want your Reticulated Python to grow. When your Reticulated Python gets older, it will not really need to eat much, but the frequency would well depend on the specie and the size of your pet.

Chapter Four: Diet and Nutrition for Reticulated Pythons

The Correct Size of Food

The prey's size that you will give to your pet Reticulated Python will heavily depend on whether or not your snake could swallow and easily digest it.

Your prey should not be wider than the widest part of your Reticulated Python's body. If the prey is too large, it could result to injuries, regurgitation, seizures, gut impactions, partial paralysis, and worse, death.

What Should I Give To My Reticulated Python?

The kind of prey that you need to give your pet varies heavily on the specie. You can ask your vet for the correct dietary requirements of your Reticulated Python, as well as the amount and frequency that you will give it.

Pre - killed vs. Live Prey

Some owners like that their snakes have the thrill of catching and hunting for live prey, such as baby chicks, mice, and rats. However, this is only a myth. Physical stimulation and metal preparation needs to come from the

Chapter Four: Diet and Nutrition for Reticulated Pythons

overall environment set-up that you will create, not through attempting to give a live animal in a small and confined space.

Some reasons why you could give pre-killed prey are the following:

- ✓ Live prey could be too active for baby snakes.
- ✓ Having live prey could permanently disfigure and scare your snake.
- ✓ If the prey attacks your Reticulated Python, it could be frightened of it; it could be very difficult for your pet to feed itself.
- ✓ Live preys that fight back could cause injuries that would include biting through the mouth area of the snake, puncturing of its eyes, and even cutting through the sheath of its tongue.

A pre-killed prey is much safer for your pet Reticulated Python. It would eliminate the possibility that your prey might gnaw and bite your snake. Chicks and mice

Chapter Four: Diet and Nutrition for Reticulated Pythons

are harmless, but rats could potentially attack and kill your pet. Aside from that mealworms and crickets would also bite and nibble on your snake.

If you really want to feed a live prey, you also need to give a food source for the prey, so it would not be tempted to eat your snake. Aside from that, watch out for any signs that would include gnawing and biting of the snakes. If this happens, immediately remove the prey and take your snake to your vet.

The dangers of a live prey could possibly be eliminated through giving pre-killed prey.

A pre-killed prey could be purchased when alive then killed by the owner, or you could already purchase an already killed prey.

After you bought the pre-killed prey, you could freeze the prey up to six months. Make sure that you thaw it completely and let it sit above room temperature before you feed it to your retic.

Chapter Four: Diet and Nutrition for Reticulated Pythons

How to Feed Pre - Killed Prey

Giving a pre-killed prey is easy; they would immediately take it and eat it. However, some snakes are picky eaters; here are some helpful tips for your snake to fully eat the prey:

- ✓ You can rub a live prey that your Reticulated Python likes to the pre-killed prey before you put it on the enclosure.
- ✓ You could also dip the prey in a warm chicken broth.

- ✓ Use hemostats or tongs to dangle the prey over the lid. Walk the prey across the cage, looking as if the prey is still alive - this would entice your snake a little bit.

- ✓ You need to ensure that your prey is warmer than the room temperature; the smell would be more appetizing for your Reticulated Python.

Chapter Four: Diet and Nutrition for Reticulated Pythons

- ✓ You can pierce your prey with a nail or pin to release scents that are more enticing for your prey.

- ✓ You can give your Reticulated Python different colored prey.

You can feed your Reticulated Python one to two times weekly; this act would result to a healthy animal as well as quick growth. However, you should reduce the food frequency and amount as it grows older. You need to give food around two to four weeks during its normal routine. Your baby Reticulated Python could eat small rats or mice.

You can start feeding your Reticulated Python a great combination of rats and mice from its infancy, this would eliminate problems especially when you constantly change prey items. When it reaches adulthood, you need change your prey to a more suitable size, such as guinea pig and rabbits.

You could even try to only give one prey at a time; this would result to an easy and swift change of food items, especially when your Reticulated Python is ready.

Chapter Four: Diet and Nutrition for Reticulated Pythons

You could also add squirrels, quail, and chicken in addition to normal preys. Feeding a full blown poultry diet would result to smelly and very runny defecation.

Your Reticulated Python is a voracious eater with a big appetite but could also be highly aggressive. This would result to a prey that needs to be only placed on feeding container or vivarium.

It is recommended that you set-up another feeding cage aside from the normal housing of your snake, however, it might not that be ideal and safe especially if your retic is too big. If you move a hunting, large snake is never a great idea, this would reduce in great injuries that can be easily avoided.

Your Retic would easily associate opening of its cage doors with food and could easily attack you at entering. Do not fret, if you handle your snake regularly this thin would not be a problem.

Chapter Four: Diet and Nutrition for Reticulated Pythons

If the attack occurs, there are methods that you can use to change the behavior:

- ✓ You can tap your Reticulated Python lightly on the head with a hook each time you open the cage if you intend to handle it. This is often called as 'tap training'. This is a popular training method.

You should never your Reticulated Python after eating; it would still be very stressful and might cause regurgitation. Do not panic if this happens, there is still no long term damage to your pet. You should let your Retic in peace before you feed it again; your pet still needs time to rebuild all the digestive fluid.

Do not handle anything that your Reticulated Python might think of as a prey and then approach to handle the snake; this would result as you being mistaken as the food.

Chapter Four: Diet and Nutrition for Reticulated Pythons

General Feeding Guidelines:

- ✓ Always provide prey for your Reticulated Python. It does not matter if it is alive or pre-killed. You should thaw it with warm water before you feed it to your snake.

- ✓ You could introduce the pre-killed, frozen, or thawed prey slowly. You need to introduce the food slowly, if it gets a little too choosy, you need to supply live food for your pet as an alternative.

- ✓ You need to provide food for your pet regularly. You could give food to it every seven to 10 days. You could even space it up to two weeks if you think that your pet is overeating. Make sure that you prepare a correct feeding schedule that your pet snake would get used to it. This would also help you track its habits and growths.

- ✓ Retics are nocturnal; you could offer food during the evening or night as they are active during this time.

Chapter Four: Diet and Nutrition for Reticulated Pythons

- ✓ You can use a specific tool to encourage feeding. You need to keep a good distance when providing food, such as tongs. Make sure you only give it in small movements to get the prey's attention. Do not force your Retic to eat the prey, or bump it into its head.

- ✓ Give a water bowl for your pet. You should always give a clean drinking water. Make sure that the dish is large yet easy to clean. Also make sure that it could not be tipped easily. Replenish the water daily to avoid contamination.

These are just some reminders on the feeding guidelines on how to create the correct and healthy diet for your Reticulated Python. Make sure to follow these steps because these are vital things to help your pet to have a happy and healthy life.

Chapter Four: Diet and Nutrition for Reticulated Pythons

Chapter Five: Starting a Family

Pet breeding is a difficult yet fulfilling task. You get to see the lineage of your pet right before your very eyes. Aside from that, you will see the greatness of the gift of life.

This should be the main point for breeding. You should not breed because you want to earn money from your pet. Remember, you will not earn that much from pet breeding. Aside from that, you would just risk the health of your pet and its future offspring if you do this task.

If you are still motivated to breed your pet, midst all the trouble and monetary trouble you will go through, we will help you with the task.

Chapter Five: Starting a Family

Truth be told, breeding is a difficult task. In this chapter, we will be your helping hand in this journey of breeding your Reticulated Python.

The Basics of Breeding

When it is still in its wild habitat, the Reticulated Python is expected to breed from September until November. These months are the interim period after the dry season and before the wet season begin. Just like any other pythons, your Reticulated Python is oviparous which means they would lay their eggs and then later on brood them. There are 87 incubation days with the standard temperature of 90 degrees F.

When in captivity, your Reticulated Python can breed regardless of the season. There are reticulated pythons that are hatched every month of the year; your male python could easily fertilize many female pythons. However, males would fiercely fight other males, so make sure that you keep these separate.

Chapter Five: Starting a Family

Sexual Maturity

Male pythons would soon be sexually mature between the ages of 12 to 18 months; the ideal length is around nine to 10 feet.

Females, on the other hand, should be around 2 1/2 to 3 years of age, with the ideal length of 13 feet.

Rule of thumb, the larger the female is, the better. However, the pythons should not be obese. An obese python is not really a good breeder.

Mimicking the Environment

When in captivity, you need to set a standard cycle for your Reticulated Python propagation. During fall, you need to slowly drop the ambient night time temperatures; also, you need to shorten the day time light. This task would lead to your females becoming "ready" to breed and she will not eat any food. However, there are still female Reticulated Pythons that would eat. At this point, the female would not show any interest in breeding. If this happens, there would not be any breeding because mainly, females are much

Chapter Five: Starting a Family

larger than males and other than that, if she does not want to, she will not release any needed pheromones that is used to attract males. This is somehow truer to less experienced males.

An experienced male could try to breed the female, but it would surely not happen. If the female does not want to breed, even with the presence of a male, it would immediately display her displeasure. She might begin violently whipping her tail back and for or even some tail wagging. Other than that, she might also push the male around using her sizable coils; she might also slam him into the walls of the enclosure. This could also happen with 'in season' females, do not be discouraged, and just remove the male immediately.

You will immediately know the difference between a severe and slight reaction from your female. If you see an adverse reaction from your female and she does not eat, you can introduce the male slowly.

Chapter Five: Starting a Family

Male Interaction

You can initially leave the male with the female around 15 to 20 minutes. For the next coming days, you can leave him a little longer until the female is more used to him.

Do not put two animals together and leave them. You must put the male with the female if you could observe the pets if they would tolerate each other.

However, take caution if the snakes are mis-sexed, such as two males being together, because this would result to a combat.

Photo cycling and temperature change is somehow unnecessary to breed Reticulated Pythons. In some case, the females would just stop eating and then be ready to breed.

In some case, if you introduce the male slowly for a short period of time, then several times over the coming weeks, the female would become ready to breed.

Males are always ready to breed if they know that they have an 'in season' female with them. The male could distinctive know this through the release of the female's pheromones.

Chapter Five: Starting a Family

In any possible case, the female Reticulated Python should have a designated basking spot in the cage, with the temperature of 90 to 95 degrees F.

The eggs should not feel temperatures above 91 degrees F, but the basking spot should be slightly warmer than 91.

For the breeding process, you need to move the male to the female enclosure. The male would investigate the female through tongue flicking. Other than that, the male would also move its lower quarter on the top of the females; he could also loosely wrap the tail around the female. Eventually, the male would be comfortable to insert one of his hemi-penes.

The actual copulation would take place for minutes or even hours. Some snake pairs would even do it non-stop at all hours of the days for weeks on time, while some pairs would just breed during the night. Some pairs have bred without being seen by the humans.

If you want to breed your Male retic to many females, you could move him at any schedule that you like. Some owners would leave a male with a specific female every five to six days, while some might move the male every day or every other day, as long as you could see that the male is not actively breeding with the female.

Some breeders stressed out that the constant moving of the males with different partners would result to increase desirability of the male. More females would desire and accept the male as its mate readily.

You need to separate all your pythons and offer food as needed. Males would easily accept the food during the breeding season only if you keep the male in another cage, away from the female. Females, in general, would never accept the food. Males eat periodically during breeding season and can breed more and still maintain a healthy body weight.

The Ovulation Process

During ovulation, there would be a mid-body swelling in the female body. This would only happen for a day or two. When the female has successfully ovulated, the male companion is not really that necessary anymore. However, if you can't see the ovulation, you can assume that ovulation has not occurred yet, so you need to constantly

Chapter Five: Starting a Family

have the male on hand. Ovulation is very easy to miss because females are generally larger than its male counterpart.

Your female retic will lay on their sides or back during gravid. This is a sure sign of pregnancy. During this stage, your female would refuse food and would just spend more time in the basking spot. Another tell - tale sign is skin shedding.

When the female has successfully lay her eggs, she would start exploring the cage and become very restless. She will find a very suitable spot to lay her eggs in. During the egg laying process, the females are usually in a trance. She does not mind the outside world. This is common, but not 100% true in all cases.

She will not mind if you take her eggs away from her, so you need to take the eggs as soon as possible if you want to incubate the eggs yourself. There is only a small chance for you to separate the eggs before it fully hardens and sticks together. A 35 to 40 retic eggs that are stuck to each other is not really an easy fit in a typical incubator. Separating these eggs would easily damage it, especially if you tear it apart.

Chapter Five: Starting a Family

If the female has finished giving birth, as well as you have taken the eggs away, you may now remove the female from the basking cage. Some females would easily allow to be grabbed while some fight you off. When doing this, you need to have a partner ready for the task. One would hold the back of her head while one would remove the body from the pile. Make sure not to disturb the eggs too much because they are very fragile. Do not roll, bump, or drop them.

At this point, you need to concern yourself greatly with the eggs. You need to leave the eggs temporarily and mix the vermiculite, or you can do this before you remove the eggs and the female. Mix the vermiculite until it can be clumped together like a snowball.

Add more water using a cup and mix it with your clean hands, until all the water is mixed thoroughly with the vermiculite. If you are quite unsure, the mixture is probably too dry than it is too wet. Both of these are a problem, you can remix and add more water or even increase the humidity. Remember, you can't remove water from the mixture and a wet egg has difficulty in fighting fungal infection.

Chapter Five: Starting a Family

Keep the humidity around 70% in the incubator. Make sure that the eggs should not collapse until they are ready to hatch. If they collapse prematurely, the eggs would be likely too dry. You need to remove them and add more water to the mixture, and increase the humidity as well.

The egg boxes are now ready and are mixed with vermiculite, you need now to put the eggs. You need to allot a space for each egg inside of it, also, do not rotate or roll the eggs too much. Some owners would mark the top of the egg, so you know which part of the egg above the vermiculite mixture.

You can even use the candle method to the eggs to know if they are really viable. You just use a small flashlight and hold it against the eggs. Turn off all the lights and the inside of the eggs will be seen. You should see a network of red veins to know that these are viable. If you are unsure, make sure that you also incubate them.

To know if it is a bad egg, you could see it on a matter of days, because it will shrivel up and become severely discolored. Your eggs should be white and fairly uniform when you see them.

Chapter Five: Starting a Family

At this stage, you need to bury your eggs about half of the way in the vermiculite, space them well so they are not too close together. This would prevent fungal infection and it would not spread the infection to other eggs.

You could also poke a few holes in the egg boxes for gas exchange, however, some people do not. You do not need to open the boxes too much because the condition inside are near perfect and you do not want to disrupt both the air temperature and the humidity level inside. However, you still need to check the box from time to time, to see if it is too dry so you can easily fix it.

You now need to put the boxes inside the incubator; you need to have a thermometer ready in each box. You need to monitor the temperature without disrupting the incubator. Close the door and let the waiting begin.

Reasons Why You Should Incubate the Eggs Artificially:

- ✓ Females won't eat until the babies are hatched. This means another three months without food for your female.
- ✓ Eggs are more likely to hatch in a controlled environment.

Chapter Five: Starting a Family

You could still let your female retic incubate the eggs herself. In this scenario, you need to have a temperature around 91 degrees F. Keep the humidity around 70%. Your retic has a natural instinct on doing this, however, this would not yield a 100% hatching rate every time.

When your eggs are safely inside the incubator, you could now give your attention back to your female retic. You could soak your female Reticulated Python with some slightly soapy water. This technique calms them down as well as removes the scent from her coils. During the soaking process, you can remove the substrate, clean the cage thoroughly and put fresh substrate on it. Rinse the soap away from the female and return it to the enclosure.

It is normal for some females to not eat again until it sheds again or if they can still smell their eggs.

After a long incubation period, your baby pythons would slowly slit the eggs open using their tooth. They would still like to inside the egg because it is more comfortable and safe inside. You should let them emerge on their own.

Chapter Five: Starting a Family

Once they go out, you need to set them aside with a moist paper towel as their substrate. This would aid them in ridding themselves of the contents of the egg that is stuck to them.

Baby pythons would shed ten days after hatching. When they shed, you need to offer them food. You can offer rat pups at first or even thawed frozen rat pups.

You need to dip the thawed prey in hot water to stimulate the smell of your retics.

What to do now with your baby pythons? Why not gift it to your snake loving friends so they could experience the joy too!

These are just some of the basic things that you need to know about breeding your Reticulated Python. These are tedious tasks and we suggest you prepare ahead of time especially the things and the cages that you need.
Still, you need some assistance in this process, we can never be too sure when your snakes are going to mate, it is best when someone is still watching your pythons during this process

Chapter Five: Starting a Family

Chapter Six: Health Care for Reticulated Pythons

Just like any living being, your Reticulated Python might experience some health problems throughout its long life. Do not fret as we will help you in this journey. Remember, you should not leave your pet Reticulated Snake alone. This chapter will introduce to you the common medical problems that you might encounter soon enough.

Chapter Six: Health Care for Reticulated Pythons

Common Health Conditions

For your reticulated python, there are so-called 'real' diseases and there are 'lay' diseases. The latter diseases are just a simple name of varied medical conditions with the same symptoms.

Many diseases have the same signs; viral, bacterial, or fungal lung infection could cause a lot of respiratory signs. These are also present in lung worms, lung mites, lung cancer, heart failure, and lung abscesses. These things are very different and need different treatment.

You need to have a stable relationship with your vet to also get a regular check-up for your Reticulated Python. Remember, it is better to prevent problems than to treat the disease once they are present.

A constant vet check-up would eradicate your fear that your snake might contract disease that is not just harmful to you but also your family.

Chapter Six: Health Care for Reticulated Pythons

Lack of Appetite or Anorexia

This is one of the most common conditions that can be seen in reticulated pythons. However, Anorexia is not a disease; this is a symptom that something else is different with your snake.

If there are deficiencies in husbandry, such as temperature, housing, humidity, lighting, and nutrition, this might be the cause of your snake Anorexia. Other causes could be trauma, or any physical event that could hurt your snake like a broken jaw could give enough pain that your retic would not like to eat.

When your retic become anorexic, you should not force feed it. Unlike people, they would not be cured if they eat. Food could support and even help your Reticulated Snake to recover from the illness; however, you still need to see the underlying cause for your Reticulated Python to have a complete recovery.

Regurgitation or Vomiting

Another common condition among retics is the vomiting. Regurgitation means that the food is removed

Chapter Six: Health Care for Reticulated Pythons

from the stomach or even above. Vomiting means that the food is expelled from the lower GI tract or below the stomach. There might be little distinction, but there is a lot of difference between the two.

Common causes:
- ✓ Management or husbandry problems
- ✓ Low humidity levels as well as low temperature in the environment
- ✓ Handling the reticulated python after it has eaten

Luckily, this thing is easily diagnosed. You should have a thorough examination of both the management and husbandry practices, and it should reveal the problem.

You could ask your vet for a thorough check of the habitat. However, there are still a lot of different causes for the vomiting or regurgitation. Some disease could cause your Reticulated Python regurgitate or even vomit after the meal include fungal and bacterial infection, parasites, viruses, cancer, obstruction, liver, pancreatic, and kidney disease, or even brain damage.

Chapter Six: Health Care for Reticulated Pythons

The diagnosis of this condition could be a simple examination of the fecal sample or as difficult as performing different lab tests or an MRI. However, these last two tests are quite pricey.

If your snake is regurgitating or even vomiting, you should thoroughly review the husbandry of the area. If all is well in the habitat, take your reticulated python to the vet for a better physical test.

Mouth Rot or Infectious Stomatitis

Mouth rot, or even infectious stomatitis is not a primary disease. This refers to any condition that affects your Reticulated Python's gums and teeth.

Just like with anorexia, mouth rot is an outcome of other disease that has a general yet serious condition. The mouth rot happens to your Reticulated Python when it is immunocompromised or even stressed due to some other cause.

Mouth Rot could also be an outcome of an injury such as in rostral trauma, or when your retic rubs the cage with its nose and bites from their prey.

Chapter Six: Health Care for Reticulated Pythons

There should be a thorough physical examination to have a both proper diagnosis and treatment. This exam would have a more hands-on evaluation. There would be lab testing, bacterial cultures, and even x-rays.

With all efforts exerted, you should still seek the opinion of a vet to have a thorough diagnosis and treatment before you do any home remedies.

Pneumonia in Retics

Respiratory refers to an ailment that involves the airways, lung, or even the nasal cavity. The respiratory ailment could range from a simple stuffy nose up to fulminate pneumonia.

In most cases, when they have presented their Reticulated Python to their vets, they are already suffering from an even advanced disease.

The most common sign for sick retic is nasal discharge, or a snotty nose. The nasal discharge could be a simple upper respiratory problem that could be easily treated with antibiotic. In some times, this discharged could

Chapter Six: Health Care for Reticulated Pythons

be an even more part of progressed disease that is associated with pneumonia in the lower respiratory tract.

Unfortunately, pneumonia is a very serious disease that could result to a high mortality.

Infections in the respiratory system of the snake could be found in the nostrils, trachea (wind pipe), lungs, and even air sacs.

Your snake does not have a diaphragm and can't cough; so if your reticulated python's lungs fill with fluid, a great example would be pus, it would have difficulty in breathing.

The sick snake would display itself from the cage with its head and neck held up, and with its mouth open. Gravity works wonders in keeping the pulmonary fluids in different proportion of the lung. This would keep the airway open to allow easy breathing. However, this is a great sign of a sick retic.

If your snake is open-mouth breathing, this is never always normal. If this happens, this could be either because of severe pain, GI disease, or even a respiratory problem.

Chapter Six: Health Care for Reticulated Pythons

Poor husbandry is the root cause of many respiratory problems. A great example is if your Reticulated Python does not have a POTZ, or the preferred optimal temperature zone, your pet could be stressed. Aside from this, this could also affect the immune system of your retic soon enough, it will transform into a disease. Without a great immune system, the retic's body can't attack and defeat all the bacteria or disease causing problems such as fungi, viruses, bacteria, and parasites.

You can treat many respiratory ailments using humidity; however, it may also be a factor for many other problems.

A great challenge posed to the vet faces is figuring out the root cause of the respiratory disease and also the incidental findings that is not really that important/

Some snakes with respiratory problems respond well to antibiotics, however, it is not really sure if every snake problem could be solved by antibiotics. A thorough physical is needed to determine the cause if your snake has a refractory respiratory ailment.

Chapter Six: Health Care for Reticulated Pythons

Some needed tests are sensitivity testing, cytology, bacterial culture, x-rays, and bacterial culture. In some cases, a CT, MRI, or even an endoscopy could be used to know the cause of the disease. Your vet could also do viral screenings and blood tests as diagnostic aids. This task is done if you have many snakes in your collection.

Retained Eye Cap or also known as Dysecdysis

Dysecdysis, or the retained eye caps and improper shedding or your reticulated python is a grave symptom of a problem, not a primary problem itself. In simpler terms, this is a symptom, not the disease.

Ecdysis or also known as the skin shedding is a dynamic task that occurs during the lifetime of your pet Reticulated Python. If your snake is already done with one shed cycle, a new cycle will begin. This is a repetitive process until your snake dies.

Retained Eye Caps in is fairly common to snakes, especially if they have problems with their shed cycles.

If your snake is healthy, the skin will shed in a single piece, which looks like a sock that is inverted. The length of

Chapter Six: Health Care for Reticulated Pythons

the shedding of your pet depends on a lot of factors; these are age and nutritional state.

A younger snake with a great diet plan would shed more than an ordinary snake. A growing and healthy snake is expected to shed at least once a month.

It takes seven to 14 days is the average sloughing of the old skin; this is the first step of the skin's shedding. Initially, the skin would be dull. After a bit, the skin could be dull and your pet's eyes may turn whitish blue. In this case, the stage is also called "opaque" or "in the blue".

At this stage, your snake would not like any food. Any other underlying skin is not yet developed at this stage, and do not handle the snake as this could cause damage to the new skin.

After three to four days, the skin would look shiny and the eyes would look clear. However, the skin could still be easily damaged through rough handling, so take good care when you are touching the animal. By the end of this phase, your snake would opt to go to rough objects, such as rocks or branches, which would start the shedding process.

Chapter Six: Health Care for Reticulated Pythons

Your skin would continually rub the skin from the tip of its nose as well as its lower jaw. It would continue to rub its skin on the cage furniture until the skin is snagged on an object. If this occurs, the snake would crawl through the remainder of the skin, it will invert its back over the body as it moves along. The final shed is complete, but it is inverted snake skin.

When your snake sheds its skin, you should check the other parts of its body, just like the eye caps or spectacles, make sure this comes off during the shedding.

The spectacles are also the clear eyelids which protect the corneas of the snake from damage. If the eye cap is retained or gets stuck, the eye would become infected.

In reality, the root cause of the shedding problem is due to management and husbandry problems. Another issue of shedding problem could cause damage in developing a new skin. This would result to dysecdysis.

Some other factors that could cause improper shedding would include:

- ✓ Low humidity

Chapter Six: Health Care for Reticulated Pythons

- ✓ Low cage temperature
- ✓ Improper nutrition
- ✓ Lacking of cage furniture for rubbing such as rocks or logs.

If these problems are corrected, the shedding process would return to normal. You need bring your snake to your vet if the changes in husbandry and management techniques do not change the dysecdysis problem.

There are some other cases concerning the dysecdysis. Some are less common, these are:

- ✓ Fungal skin diease
- ✓ Mites
- ✓ Systemic disease
- ✓ Septicemia
- ✓ Microfilaria (parasites)
- ✓ Old scars
- ✓ Thermal burns

Because these are different, you may need to contact your vet immediately for proper assessment.

Chapter Six: Health Care for Reticulated Pythons

Acariasis

Acariasis, also known as the infestation of mites and ticks, should not be treated as a nuisance. This infestation is usually associated to diseases and could cause a costly problem in the future.

Luckily, once you identified the ectoparasite, the acariasis can be easily treated.

Ophionyssus Natricis, also called as the snake mite, is the most common ectoparasite in snake. Adult males of this mite are hematophagous, which means they suck blood. When they form large numbers, they could debilitate the snake through a life-threatening anemia. Aside from that, these mites could act as vectors of different disease when they travel from animal to animal, or even cage to cage.

Snake mites could easily travel between the scales, around the folds of the snake's eye caps, and even the labial pits.

Unsanitary cage conditions, recent acquisitions o imports, and poor husbandry practices are some commonly things associated with Acariasis.

Chapter Six: Health Care for Reticulated Pythons

These mites could easily enter a newly acquired animal if they have not been quarantined properly. When you have put the snake on a cage, these mites could easily spread to other animals in your household.

This snake mite, also called the acariasis, could be an agent of infectious snake diseases such as Leukocytozoon, Aeromonas hydrophila, and other hematozoans.

Aeromonas hydrophilia is one of the common causes associated to infectious stomatitis, or mouth rot, and pneumonia. There have been also speculations of these things being transmitted to different snakes, but has not been proven yet.

The mite infestation could be subtle, which means that the mites are hiding under the skin folds of the jaw or to even obvious, mites that cover the entire animals in addition to other mites crawling on the cage.

These mites vary greatly in color depending on its specie, sex of the mite, its age, and how recently it has eaten or taken blood.

If your Reticulated Python has a mite infestation, it would usually have a lackluster and dull appearance. Mites

Chapter Six: Health Care for Reticulated Pythons

typically stay on the specific area of he Reticulated Python's body where it could have the most protection from the outside world. Under the child or gular folds, the periocular regions around the eyes, under the scutes, and inside the skin folds around the cloaca are some areas that mites could accumulate.

When they appear in large groups, both ticks and mites are very difficult to erase. Ectoparasites are a great source of debilitation and disease, even in an individual pet. Do not fret, these parasites are easily diagnosed, and if you use the correct plan, it could be easily exterminated.

The most important thing to do here is to treat not just the snake, but the entire room/cage/facility. If the cage is not treated along with the snake, ticks and mites could easily come back.

You need to immediately call your vet for the proper treatment for the ticks. Some home remedies might be toxic not just to the pest but also to the patient.

Chapter Six: Health Care for Reticulated Pythons

Stress for your Reticulated Python

Stress appears different reasons. In some cases, the cause of stress may feel threatened, being handled improperly handled or too often, no place to hide, or even living in substandard conditions. See if these things are present in the current environment.

Luckily, most of these things can be easily reduced or even eliminated through giving the proper care for your Reticulated Python. Good snake care is the best thing to do to fight against diseases and illnesses that could affect your snake.

You can't easily stress your snake; however, the stress could build up and produce other symptoms. These symptoms are weight loss, refusal to eat, lethargy, or in worst case possible, and death.

You can't see stress in snakes the way you can see other health problems, such as external parasites or a retained shed. But stress can "build up" in snakes to produce other symptoms like the refusal to eat, weight loss, lethargy, and, in extreme cases, even death.

Chapter Six: Health Care for Reticulated Pythons

As the owner, you need to be the one to know the cause of the stress and find ways to reduce or even eradicate it.

Create a conducive environment for your snake. Make sure to pay close attention to things such as hiding spots, temperatures, fresh water, substrates, and etc. If you have given a proper environment, this would typically reduce stress as well as other health problems. Aside from that, you should not handle your pet too often. If you over handle your pet in an improper environment, this would create stress for your Reticulated Python.

Although snakes are big and vicious creatures, your snake is still afraid with the big scary world out there.

Dehydration

Dehydration could gravely affect your snakes in different ways. Some are mild while some are severe. Fortunately, they are fairly easy to prevent.

A problem in shedding is a typical sign of dehydration. To prevent this problem, you need to ensure that the Reticulated Python has clean drinking water easily

Chapter Six: Health Care for Reticulated Pythons

available and accessible. Water is the cause and primary solution for dehydration for your retics.

Aside from that, you should track the humidity levels in the cage, especially where the snake is located. Your retic needs a specific humidity level to shed properly and to stay hydrated.

If you are living in a low-humidity and dry area, you need to create artificial humidity for your pet, especially during its shed cycle. You can use an ordinary household humidifier or even a moisture retreat for your snake inside the cage. Research thoroughly on the specific humidity level that your Retic needs in order to survive.

These are just some of the things that you need to know about the health concerns of the Reticulated Python. These are just some initial items that could affect your pet. However, you still need to consult your vet if there is something wrong with the pet.

Remember, prevention is better than cure. Have regular check-up to see even the tiniest problems before it turns into a big problem.

Chapter Seven: Handling Your Reticulated Pythons (Optional)

The Reticulated Python is an amazing pet for you to have. It would be with you for a long time yet it is still relatively low maintenance. We have thoroughly discussed its rich history as well as the things to know if you want to take care of it. For this last chapter, we'll give you some handling tips if ever you wish to handle your pet pythons. We hope that you have learned a lot from this short yet concise book about the Retics. These are just some essential information that you need to know about the Reticulated Python. There are so much more to learn about these fantastic creatures!

Chapter Seven: Handling Your Reticulated Pythons

Can I Handle My Reticulated Python?

Optional Method

It is normal for them to hide or defend themselves, but they cannot really harm you (since they are non – venomous) unless of course you sort of taunt them. What you need to do as soon as your snake arrives especially in the first few days is to just let them roam around the house (supervised) for about an hour each day and allow your pet to get used to your smell.

Give your new pet a few weeks to settle into its home and get used to a regular feeding routine. Remember, snakes are also living beings that need to settle and get used to new spaces. The end of this initial week, you can now begin to move things around inside your snake's terrarium. However, it is still not allowed to attempt to touch your pet python at this point. Continuously do this for another week so that your snake can get used to the idea that you have no intention to harm him.

Being around it without attempting to touch it will let your Reticulated python know that you are not a danger or

Chapter Seven: Handling Your Reticulated Pythons

threat. Once you think that your snake know that you are not a threat, you can start to touch it while inside its cage by placing your hand in its cage and gently start touching it, moving it around inside the cage, and lifting your snake's tail. Continue doing this manner to your snake for three to four days.

Once you see that your pet is comfortable with its new surroundings, you can start approaching your snake. However, do not handle it for the first two to three days after a meal.

Avoid handling it as if you're a predator as what predators do is that they would approach it from the top, so do it from the side. Then slowly but confidently lift it. Hesitation will scare your snake and will cause it to hide or bite. When your Reticulated python realizes you are not going to eat it, it will calm down and tame quickly. Eventually, it will become used to handling.

Chapter Seven: Handling Your Reticulated Pythons

Conclusion

You could still search the web for more details about this species. What we have given you is just a detailed insight; we hope you have learned a lot from this short but informative book. What better thing to do now? Go out and purchase your very first Reticulated Python! Enjoy!

Glossary of Snake Terms

1.2.3. (Numbers with full stops) – The numbers are used to denote the number of a species, arranged according to sex, thus: male.female.unknown sex. In this case, one male, two females, and three of unknown sex.

Acclimation – Adjusting to a new environment or new conditions over a period of time.

Active range – The area of activity which can include hunting, seeking refuge, and finding a mate.

Ambient temperature – The overall temperature of the environment.

Amelanistic – Amel for short; without melanin, or without any black or brown coloration.

Anal Plate – A modified ventral scale that covers and protects the vent; sometimes a single plate, sometimes a divided plate.

Anerythristic – Anery for short; without any red coloration.

Aquatic – Lives in water.

Arboreal – Lives in trees.

Betadine – An antiseptic that can be used to clean wounds in reptiles.

Bilateral – Where stripes, spots or markings are present on both sides of an animal.

Biotic – The living components of an environment.

Brille – A transparent scale above the eyes of snakes that allows them to see but also serves to protect the eyes at the same time. Also called Spectacle, and Ocular Scale.

Brumation – The equivalent of mammalian hibernation among reptiles.

Cannibalistic – Where an animal feeds on others of its own kind.

Caudocephalic Waves – The ripple-like contractions that move from the rear to the front of a snake's body.

CB – Captive Bred, or bred in captivity.

CH – Captive Hatched.

Cloaca – also Vent; a half-moon shaped opening for digestive waste disposal and sexual organs.

Cloacal Gaping – Indication of sexual receptivity of the female.

Cloacal Gland – A gland at the base of the tail which emits foul smelling liquid as a defense mechanism; also called Anal Gland.

Clutch – A batch of eggs.

Constriction – The act of wrapping or coiling around a prey to subdue and kill it prior to eating.

Crepuscular – Active at twilight, usually from dusk to dawn.

Crypsis – Camouflage or concealing.

Diurnal – Active by day

Drop – To lay eggs or to bear live young.

Ectothermic – Cold-blooded. An animal that cannot regulate its own body temperature, but sources body heat from the surroundings.

Endemic – Indigenous to a specific region or area.

Estivation – Also Aestivation; a period of dormancy that usually occurs during the hot or dry seasons in order to escape the heat or to remain hydrated.

Faunarium (Faun) – A plastic enclosure with an air holed lid, usually used for small animals such as hatchling snakes, lizards, and insects.

FK – Fresh Killed; a term usually used when feeding a rodent that is recently killed, and therefore still warm, to a pet snake.

Flexarium – A reptile enclosure that is mostly made from mesh screening, for species that require plenty of ventilation.

Fossorial – A burrowing species.

Fuzzy – For rodent prey, one that has just reached the stage of development where fur is starting to grow.

F/T – Frozen/thawed; used to refer to food items that are frozen but thawed before feeding to your pet.

Gestation – The period of development of an embryo within a female.

Gravid – The equivalent of pregnant in reptiles.

Glottis – A tube-like structure that projects from the lower jaw of a snake to facilitate ingestion of large food items.

Gut-loading – Feeding insects within 24 hours to a prey before they are fed to your pet, so that they pass on the nutritional benefits.

Hatchling – A newly hatched, or baby, reptile.

Hemipenes – Dual sex organs; common among male snakes.

Hemipenis – A single protrusion of a paired sexual organ; one half is used during copulation.

Herps/Herpetiles – A collective name for reptile and amphibian species.

Herpetoculturist – A person who keeps and breeds reptiles in captivity.

Herpetologist – A person who studies ectothermic animals, sometimes also used for those who keeps reptiles.

Herpetology – The study of reptiles and amphibians.

Hide Box – A furnishing within a reptile cage that gives the animal a secure place to hide.

Hots – Venomous.

Husbandry – The daily care of a pet reptile.

Hygrometer – Used to measure humidity.

Impaction – A blockage in the digestive tract due to the swallowing of an object that cannot be digested or broken down.

Incubate – Maintaining eggs in conditions favorable for development and hatching.

Interstitial – The skin between scales.

Intromission – Also mating; when the male's hemipenis is inserted into the cloaca of the female.

Juvenile – Not yet adult; not of breedable age.

LTC – Long Term Captive; or one that has been in captivity for more than six months.

MBD – Metabolic Bone Disease; occurs when reptiles lack sufficient calcium in their diet.

Morph – Color pattern

Musking – Secretion of a foul smelling liquid from its vent as a defense mechanism.

Oviparous – Egg-bearing.

Ovoviviparous – Eggs are retained inside the female's body until they hatch.

Pinkie – Newborn rodent.

Pip – The act of a hatchling snake to cut its way out of the egg using a special egg tooth.

PK – Pre-killed; a term used when live rodents are not fed to a snake.

Popping – The process by which the sex is determined among hatchlings.

Probing – The process by which the sex is determined among adults.

Regurgitation – Also Regurge; occurs when a snake regurgitates or brings out a half-digested meal.

R.I. – Respiratory Infection; common condition among reptiles kept in poor conditions.

Serpentine Locomotion – The manner in which snakes move.

Sloughing – Shedding.

Sub-adult – Juvenile.

Substrate – The material lining the bottom of a reptile enclosure.

Stat – Short for Thermostat

Tag – Slang for a bite or being bitten

Terrarium – A reptile enclosure.

Thermo-regulation – The process by which cold-blooded animals regulate their body temperature by moving from hot to cold surroundings.

Vent – Cloaca

Vivarium – Glass-fronted enclosure

Viviparous – Gives birth to live young.

WC – Wild Caught.

Weaner – A sub-adult rodent.

WF – Wild Farmed; refers to the collection of a pregnant female whose eggs or young were hatched or born in captivity.

Yearling – A year old.

Zoonosis – A disease that can be passed from animal to man.

Photo Credits

Page 1 Photo by user Michael via Flickr.com, https://www.flickr.com/photos/45018899@N00/383444766/

Page 5 Photo by user Karin Lewis (Bookatz via Flickr.com, https://www.flickr.com/photos/karinlewis/32599977410/

Page 14 Photo by user Tom Jutte via Flickr.com, https://www.flickr.com/photos/hereistom/26230096290/

Page 27 Photo by user jinjian liang via Flickr.com, https://www.flickr.com/photos/liangjinjian/3453347453/

Page 58 Photo by user Ruth Ellison via Flickr.com, https://www.flickr.com/photos/laruth/2911290131/

Page 72 Photo by user Heather Paul via Flickr.com, https://www.flickr.com/photos/warriorwoman531/8129432457/

Page 86 Photo by user Thailandecoportal.com via Flickr.com, https://www.flickr.com/photos/thailandecoportal/4763689226/

Page 105 Photo by user Stephen Collins via Flickr.com, https://www.flickr.com/photos/trib/7052912915/

References

"Reticulated Python Care Sheet" - ReptilesMagazine.com

http://www.reptilesmagazine.com/Care-Sheets/Snakes/Reticulated-Python/

"Life History - ReticulatedPython.info

http://www.reticulatedpython.info/h4.html

"Python reticulatusReticulated Python" - AnimalDiversity.org

http://animaldiversity.org/accounts/Python_reticulatus/

"Python reticulatus" - ITIS.gov

https://www.itis.gov/servlet/SingleRpt/SingleRpt?search_topic=TSN&search_value=209567#null

"Reticulated python" - ReptilePark.com

https://reptilepark.com.au/animals/reptiles/snakes/exotic-snakes/reticulated-python/

"Reticulated python" - SnakeType.com

https://www.snaketype.com/reticulated-python/

"Reticulated Python Care Tips" - ReptilesMagazine.com

http://www.reptilesmagazine.com/Snakes/Snake-Care/Reticulated-Python-Care-Tips/

"Snake Habitats, How to Create" - Drsfostersmith.com

https://www.drsfostersmith.com/pic/article.cfm?articleid=2383

"Reticulated Python" - Python reticulatus

Petmd.com

https://www.petmd.com/reptile/species/reticulated-python#

"8 Bedding Options for Your Pet Snake" - TheSprucePets.com

https://www.thesprucepets.com/bedding-options-for-pet-snake-2662258

"How Often Should I Clean My Reptile's Habitat?" - AnimalCityInc.com

https://animalcityinc.com/blog/44713/how-often-should-i-clean-my-reptiles-habitat

"Habitats: Cleaning and Disinfecting Reptile Cages" - PetCoach.co

https://www.petcoach.co/article/habitats-cleaning-and-disinfecting-reptile-cages/

"How to Clean a Snake Cage Quickly and Easily" - ReptileKnowledge.com

http://www.reptileknowledge.com/news/how-to-clean-a-snake-cage-quickly-and-easily/

"Maintenance" - Reticulatedpython.info

http://reticulatedpython.info/c4.html

"Common Health Problems in Snakes" - ReptileKnowledge.com

http://www.reptileknowledge.com/care/snake-health.php

"Breeding Retics" - Tripod.com

http://mahn001.tripod.com/id37.html

"Breeding" - Reticulatedpython.info

http://reticulatedpython.info/c10.html

"Snake Health 101" - ReptilesMagazine.com

http://www.reptilesmagazine.com/Snakes/Snake-Health-101/

"Snake Feeding Tips" - Drsfostersmith.com

https://www.drsfostersmith.com/pic/article.cfm?aid=2372

"How to Look After a Reticulated Python" - WikiHow.com

https://www.wikihow.com/Look-After-a-Reticulated-Python#Feeding_Your_Python_sub

www.ingramcontent.com/pod-product-compliance
Lightning Source LLC
Chambersburg PA
CBHW060839050426
42453CB00008B/751